The Third Symphony

Dancing on the Strings of Love

Nadia Abu Shama

Dr. M. E. Fayad

@2024 AEEH PRESS INC

Middle East Manager and Editor: Ahmed M. Shalaby

Cover Design: Mahmoud Assad

Translation: *Ashraf Abdel Hamid Al Genbihy*

This book, mixing and sharing collaborative thoughts and love letters together, is the most charming short story ever conceived in the authors' imaginations.

AEEH PRESS INC

Brilliant Stars in the Sky of Literature and Writing

My sophisticated erudite student, Nadia Abu Shama, is of Algerian origin. She is a distinguished writer, an eloquent first-class person, and a talented writer. In a fantasy world other than that one you live, you are under a spell with her charming words, dancing with her messages. She is able to stir up all the sorrows confined in your deep recesses, so as to perceive the universe with the eyes of purity, serenity, and childish ecstasy.

She was born and brought up in the Babur Mountains - the city hanging at the foot of a large mountain with a geographical and historical heritage and home to revolutionaries during the French occupation, where great revolutions and battles took place. This region of enchanting and rare beauty was very isolated and remote from the capital city , just like a pearl or an expensive diamond concealed from all the world's eyes.

Collaborating with Dr. Fayyad, she has written thoughts, in the form of letters, and more than forty books, "Universal Symphonies." Examples of her masterpieces are: "The Novel of Al-Taffar" , "The Nude Body," "The Legend," "Dancing on Water," "The Ram Dancer," "The Gazelle of Al-Bawadi," "The Prisoner of the Past," and "The Rape of a Woman".

0000000

Dr. Muhammad Fayyad, an American of Egyptian origin, spent more than forty years, dedicating his life to the niche of knowledge, and spending the best days of his life in fruitful scientific research. Then generations, graduated under his supervision and sponsorship, believed in the value of science and learning, which contributed indirectly to the renaissance and development of America and other countries of the world through multiple expeditionary trips to spread knowledge around the globe.

Dr. Muhammad Fayyad contributed positively and globally to raising the status of human civilization in the world and participated in composing the "Cosmic Symphonies". Among his scientific, literary and reform works, he published ten scientific and permanent books and more than 500 scientific articles in the most famous scientific journals and conferences. And add to this, his striving to spread his innovations in the "Engineering of Unified Concepts", "the Unified and Stable Linguistic Engineering", "the Engineering of the Unified Field", and "the Art of Abstraction". This is all with God's help.

Dedication

To the one who is unbridled in her feelings, the one who is rebellious, and unleashed like a ray of light that pierces all eyes and souls, not caring about the laws of men and subject only to the laws of heaven, to the one who has made me a modern emperor, and has turned my forgotten history into a tale to tell in all ages. To the one who carved my name on the list of Eternal lovers.

Nadia Abu Shama

"She thinks that I may tend to another one , love her the same.

My heart belongs to the one I love, and so does my name.

I sipped the cup of love but only once

Other than yours I've spilt; I'll have no chance."

From the "The Pulse of Famous letters"

Dr. M.E. Fayad

Table Of Contents

1

True Love

My beloved must be blessed with a strong and beautiful passion that increases his innovation and determination to succeed.

He must publish more and more books and writings than that he wrote before I was with him.

My beloved must obtain a double number of new innovations and their patents to serve humanity, and surpass what he achieved before.

My beloved must be an everlasting sun in all advanced sciences and research.

My beloved must obtain the largest unparalleled projects and run them for the benefit of humanity.

With his knowledge, innovations and inventions, he should help with the prosperity and progress of humanity seeking the help of God Almighty.

Baby I will never let you be unsuccessful I will change my way of love.

I will force my heart to wait for you in terrible silence.

I will accompany you in all the directions you desire to be the faithful friend that pushes you forward and the hug that gives you tenderness.

I will follow you like your shadow, but I will never disturb you.

I will transform my grief and my longing for positive energy in constant waiting, because your soul accompanies me wherever I am.

From now on, I will not care about you in such a crazy way except in the moments of your presence near me or being alone with me.

I will reason and calm down, even if this tears my depths and throws me into the hellfire of endless torment.

I will be the quiet one even if my depths bleed in pain due to longing for you.

I will only care about myself and my miserable words that accompany my loneliness.

I will wear the mourning outfits until I see you in front of me, until you make me take off the black mourning outfits and dress me up in all the wonderful colors of life.

 I will just write to you constantly.

Time without being with you is something like loss and vagrancy in the face of such fickle and unsteady life.

Time without being with you is like losing pleasure in the gardens of my pain.

I am no longer the one I used to be.

I have become another human being who is constantly enveloped in silence, waiting and fear.

2

How cruel it is when you have within you both wound and hope together!

How cruel it is when both wound and hope come together within you!

Strong winds blow on you, uprooting all the plants of your aching heart, to plant a new love experience in its place.

The breezes of pleasure will blow you away.

A fresh radiance will appear on your face.

Your arm will reach out to embrace all your dreams

To embrace your only love again after it has left you for many years.

How much you are in a bad need for a pure warm bosom to lay your head on!

Alas! you may cry out your eyes for every moment that has passed whilst your sad heart refuses to dance on the strings of love.

You will dance with my heart and call on my soul at the advent of night.

3

You are the dearest and most beautiful lover

You are the most invaluable and dearest lover in the world.

You are the most beautiful and tender heart that contains me. You are my most wonderful love story.

Let me dive deep into you and your love more and more.

Let's live the most blissful life together.

Let's each one of us be the other's completing half.

Let me adore you every day anew.

Every day I love you in a new way.

Let me serve you for the rest of my life because I deeply love you.

Let me draw love with all its rituals within you because known love and you have never been shaken by its storms.

With love, you will fly all over the world.

You will be much younger in age, then you will know the real life.

You will be having goose bumps in every moment of your life.

You will miss me every second.

You will embrace the whole world.

With love, you will go very happily to your work.

You will desire to come back to me.

You will scream in the face of the whole world and say," I am in complete love and passion".

I love her extremely.

My love to you will change every moment of sadness within you.

It will change every moment of silence within you.

It will change every moment of depression within you.

I want you to be like a free bird soaring in the sky of the world. You are always happy.

Simply, because I LOVE you ...

4

What a great man you are!

Your words overwhelm me whenever I hear them.

They force me to love you more.

They lead me to ecstasy when you write them to me.

Looking at your pictures drives me absolutely mad, for I am continuously in love with you.

Even in my fear of losing you, I find a mighty force within me that pushes me to joy and to you...

A mighty force that dwells within me whilst I am in your arms...

How great you are as a human being!

And how sublime you are as a lover!

And how wonderful you are as a man!

5

I let all the women of the world flirt with you

I let all the women of the world flirt with you.

I sail in all the eyes of everyone.

And I run like children in the gardens and the streets.

I walk in the rain and embrace the rainbow.

I make myself a beautiful dress studded with your love and tenderness.

You deserve the love of all women in the world.

For I trust you and I am sure that your heart will definitely guide you back to me.

No other woman will seduce you.

And no other beautiful eyes other than mine will bring you back because I …

… I simply love you, and I want you to be the best and happiest human being.

6

I wonder why the fates did keep you away from me!

Thoughts are crowding in my head whereas longings are mixing in my heart.

Sometimes I find myself sad, but at other times lonely.

I'm looking for another way to escort my dream and hope.

So, I find the way to you very long and the days are countless.

I find you in an exile other than where I am.

I'm trying to scream as loud as I can, so that you can hear my groaning, so that you can hear the pain of my heart, so you will rush to me.

Perhaps you would run to hide me in your arms, but you did not come.

How hard it is to be away from you!

And how hard it is to need you!

I wonder why fates kept you away from me?

Why did the wheel of years put you on the track of my life?

I wonder why I remained as a hostage in this space and in this distressed heart?

I wonder how long till I meet you and drink from the springs of your affection and dwell in the pathways of your love?

We resist with our might, but sometimes we feel our innate vulnerability.

We are in bad need for…... .

We see the ropes of tears wrapped around our necks.

Even words are conquered in front of our feelings, vulnerability, and needs.

I'm afraid of time…

I fear for you every step you take.

I feel a tingling pain in my heart.

Sleep is lost from my eyes, and I find the chaos of time enveloping me.

I love you and how beautiful this love is!

How cruel is your absence from me!

I want to smell your fragrant body.

To hold you with all my might.

I want to pour my kisses down on you.

I will write you a new birth certificate.

….

7

Just moments

In my moments of sadness…

In my moments of weakness…

In my moments of solitude…

In my lonely moments with you…

My cities are collapsing…

A flood is sweeping away my streets.

The feeling of nostalgia is overwhelming me.

I want to escape to any place far away from the areas of my thirst, so that I may be able to escape from the claws of longing.

So that I may live far from the places of pain…

All the music I select caresses my wounds and my depths…

I find myself very weak and in my moments of weakness I want you to be close to me…

To contain me, to hide me in the eyelids of your eyes, to make me a strong female…

To give me new confidence, new strength, and a new flame…

How miserable I am without you!

How miserable I am in your absence!

How sad are the moments of my terrible longings!

How unhappy I am when I say I will not wait for you.

I will write a lot, read a lot, and draw a lot.

I will find myself reading nothing but the cups of astrologers who read the future and foretell about you.

I only look at your palms.

I only draw pictures of your face in the evening of my presence and on the page of my eagerness.

I am unhappy without being folded in your arms!

How miserable I am without your heart!

Without your soul and without your goodness with me.

8

Writing to You

Is writing to you the real obsession?

Or is my yearning for you the strong motivation for me to write constantly.

Is it to feel the pulse of your being during the moments of your love's abscence from me?

Is it that I love writing about you?

Or is it your desire for my love to be crowned with words, to refresh your soul as you always tell me?

Are the words as sacred as love for me and for you ?

I have repeatedly tried not to become addicted to you or your being with me, not to become addicted to my love for you.

This is because I used to go crazy in everything: I used to get married with joys and soar over the borders of your distant homeland.

I used to become without an identity in the country of your laws.

When I was addicted to you, I found myself swimming in all of your fields, without exception.

I asked myself a lot of questions: Is this love indeed?

If love is with this power, ecstasy, and beauty, why are we deviated from it by so many periods of time?

Why are we destined to be lost and wandering in this empty and void world in search of our souls that have surely been dancing together in our absence?

9

Tell me how did it come that I loved you....

My lord,

Tell me how did it come that I loved you.

why did I love you?

How did I get preoccupied with you more than l did with my soul and my life?...

How did it come that you were in my life more invaluable than my life?

How did it happen that I had become unable to live without you?

I used to grieve for no reason just because I would not hear your voice.

Or just because you would not send me your letters.

Or just because you used to be busy with your work, research and all your affairs.

So, I find myself totally lost...

Distracted,

Besides, I find within myself endless pains,

I want to get rid of them all, to get them out of my inner circle.

Also, I find myself flying in a deep abyss of loss.

Even the great hope has begun to lose its strong luster in front of my eyes.

All dreams have begun to fade away.

So, sad musical tunes have preceded me to pierce my ears.

10

My Craving to You

How strange is my craving to you, indeed?

Towards your love, it strongly me does lead.

I strongly love life and everything in it for you.

With your love everything is strong, impulsive and daring.

I want you altogether with the power of things.

I want to be a little away from your altar so that you may work quietly.

However, I find myself running like an unstoppable mare.

I grow more eager, and nearer to death every moment I pretend to stay away from this path that leads me to you.

I love you violently, strongly and overwhelmingly.

Are you dying like me every moment to be with me.

You are always sighing anxiously because you are far from me.

How could you leave words stuck in my throat?

How could you leave them even compete with my whole life.

They are willing to reach you in any case.

16

They are willing to dwell with you anywhere…

Are you also broken up into small units like time while you are away from me?!

Are you also seeking to run away from all your worries and all your dates at my temple and in my arms?

Do you have the desire to hug me tight and scream at the top of your voice to say: "I love you madly, honey!"

11

To you...... ♥

Perhaps my first date with you was completely forgotten, but it was too impressive to make me recall all its details.

Whenever I go through hard times, I feel as if the end is approaching.

However, your phantom and memory used to be and will be the refuge to which you and I would leave or will leave.

I remember that one day I heard some women say that the phantoms keep going around us in a circle and we feel their presence.

However, even your phantom has inhabited the depths of my soul.

How much I dived deep in your eyes secretly.

Your tell-tale eyes repeatedly revealed everything without being asked.

It was as if revealing what was inside you was something unattainable.

However, once it came out, it spread out like a symphony tune that had overwhelmed me with joy.

I may wonder again, why, at the splendor of your word, I sit baffled like the needy in the middle of roads, having nothing of the world's possessions?

The passersby harshly bumped into me without even asking what was wrong with me.

Reply to me if you have an answer.

From my heart I give you all the affection.

I miss you so much although the meeting is near to come. ♥

12

How hard it is!

How hard it is for me to wait eagerly like hours, like the slow creeping of time, and the mumbling of the distressed heart!

How hard it is for me to carry you inside me like a newly-born babe, and to tickle the depths of my longing with the time stolen from our lives… !

I love to write for the whole world except for you…

I have no desire that you read the letters my words.

I want you to realize that I am within you.

I aspire to be freed from the castles of distance and the rituals of insolent longings.

My wish for us is to be gathered at one age, one timing, one night and one sunrise.

13

Excuse me if I have confessed to you...

Excuse me if I admitted to you that I had waited for you all night.

I was endorsed in writing.

I was diving deep into the seas of your eagerness that you would no longer disclose in front of me.

How much I liked your waiting today.

How I used to accompany you in the auditorium seats while you were showering me with your abundant knowledge, your overflowing feelings and your believing in yourself.

You used to confirm everything you gave to me.

How much happiness prevailed me!

My heart was beating violently while I was waiting to hear your voice that made me feel safe and ecstatic.

Waiting to look at the smile on your face.

And so, to have some of your smile.

Has our love matured because its passion has turned into a romantic waiting?

Or the letters of my words adorned it and made it like a groom preparing himself for the wedding night?

There is pleasure in speed and so is in delay.

It is the first time that I have found myself waiting for you.

Yet, I did not complain about my waiting.

I found myself waiting on a beautiful journey.

I felt your love expanding more in all my parts.

As for you, you were more tending to the feeling that we would be deprived of our reunion.

However, you were at the top of your giving and at the top of moments of ecstasy while you are immersed in your beautiful world. I have always dreamed of sharing this world with you and inheriting some of its legacy from you.

14

Damn Love

Damn the love that makes us fly very joyfully like birds, then brings us down to the deepest part of the earth with the weight of the pains within us.

Damn this love that always makes us in conflict with ourselves.

Damn the distances that separate lovers, one from each other.

Damn the distances that deprive them of the real life that they must live to shorten time and history and to be free from the life of illusions.

Damn the heart that bleeds just because you are away from it for hours.

Just because you are away for half a day or one whole day.

Damn the love whose arms wrap us around and make longing slaughter all our bodies' veins and arteries.

I will be killed a million times with the swords of longing.

You will plant all arrows in my dancing soul.

You will find me looking for you in all places as before.

I want you not to leave me for one single moment.

How hard it is for souls thirsting for love, adoration and attention!

How hard are the souls that have been displaced on the footways of time in search of a heart that beats for them!

In search of tender arms to contain them.

How often we inhabited barren deserts devoid of tender feelings and melodious voices that reach our ears.

We were throwing ourselves at the feet of buried sadness and happiness.

15

Commit suicide, O leaves!

O you miserable tree leaves, commit suicide!

Let the flames devour your glowing face.

Just like me, you are sitting alone at the end of night, waiting for the moon to rise.

 O you tree leaves! You are just like me.

You feel lonely and bitter at the same time.

The more you are raped by the pens, the more you rebel and flee to separate places from there.

Exactly you are like me.

Here I am retrieving the stabs of my aching heart, and repeating them with my tongue on all the ears.

In the temple of love, I wait for the hymns of the love prayer, so that I may meet you as I used to dream, as I used to crave.

What is it that going on to cut my depths and make them torn and scattered everywhere?

How cruel is it for the continents to be separated by seas and oceans.

Some of them are located at night and others during the day.

Imagine that Christopher Columbus had not discovered America, and remained unknown to us and our miserable minds, no one would have ever suffered.

A time earlier, May Ziadah[1] suffered when Gibran Khalil Gibran[2] passed away.

She suffered when he preferred living in America to his beloved with her glowing heart.

When he preferred pink dreams and the pages of various books, he left without returning.

They both kept writing to each other.

They both were overcoming distances and burning longings with clippings of love letters that lasted for many months to extinguish their flames of passion.

Despite the distances and their impossible reunion, they were sincere and loyal in their love.

Their hearts were always embracing each other.

Their souls were intertwined.

Their success was all derived from an inner strength resided in their depths.

All the outstanding innovations, in their literary works up to the moment, were caused by distances and by torment. They were caused by the separation of the two hearts and bodies.

____

[1] May Ziadah was an Arab writer who was born in Nazareth in 1886 and died in1941
[2] Gibran Khalil Gibran was a Lebanese-American writer, poet and visual artist; he was also considered a philosopher.

If, in our recent time, such a story had taken place, it would have been impossible for anyone to believe. It would have been considered as something imaginary or fabricated.

Although the world has become like a small village and everything has become attainable, everyone is alienating from one another.

The truth has become unclear and indecisive.

Sincere feelings have faded away.

There were only verses, a few songs, or some romantic films in which we would entertain ourselves.

They confronted the hard and dull feelings of this current generation.

Such generation renounced everything beautiful and smart.

It has renounced the true core of life and has gone after the chaff.

They cannot sort out the sheep from the goats.

It has lost the true essence of life.

You yourself, sir, cannot believe the burning, sincere feelings emanating from all corners of the world.

However, we can no longer understand such feelings.

We can no longer bear the pain and be patient with the fluctuations of time and the instability of our souls.

Despite all this, I cannot help but be faithful to my letters, to my heart feelings, to its successive beats.

I still love life as I loved it at the beginning of my life.

I still believe in pure feelings that are free from all falsehood, from disappointment, from all the knots of life.

I still believe in the pure feelings that drive the lover to complete liberation, to travel far beyond the seas of our beautiful eyes, to climb the walls of our trembling hearts, to step up to a point in ourselves and scream at the top of our lungs.

The feelings that push the lover to exist, to be free from himself and from us, to be free like wild birds flying high in the sky, to love strongly and develop quickly, to embrace happiness in the arms of a loving and infatuated heart, to make it a place of joy and pleasure.

It is adorned with the sparkle of transparent eyes, colored by the smiles of your sexy lips, provoked by the scent of your fragrant body, and woven by the veins of his aching heart with dangling and colored threads from all corners of your being, to decorate your present and future.

You are devouring my words as if they are biscuits coated in chocolate liquid, with cups of natural juice of various fruits.

I don't know if eating them have become a normal habit devoid of passion, love, unbridled desire, and wandering around my temple?

Or is it still transporting you to lovely worlds that you have never visited before?

Have you ever lived in such palaces that all lovers used to live in?

You no longer talk to me about them.

You no longer flirt with my soul, my inkwell, and my pens.

I am no longer silent, hiding behind the walls of many works.

I am no longer silent as one who is fleeing from oneself to oneself.

I am back as if I am searching for my amputated organ, searching for my lost heart that has been enveloped in perpetual silence and confusion.

You are searching in the caves of words and feelings for the new language spoken by your heart and chanted by the tongues of your soul.

You want a fatwa[3] for it from the masses of scholars and religious people.

You became indifferent, preoccupied with everything except for your heart.

You are trying to imprison your heart again in your usual cage. You became indifferent, caring only about the issues of peoples and sciences.

You forgot your true case, especially my case with you.

Are you always weak in front of your prisoners as you used to be at all times?

Do you always detest the approaching of shining suns towards the windows of your prison to ignite the light within you, in order to illuminate all your corners, in order to see life as it really is.

You became indifferent, cold, reserved and preoccupied with everything.

You were used to walking in all roads and streets except the one that was leading to me.

____

[3] A fatwa is a legal ruling on a point of Islamic law (sharia) given by a qualified Faqih (Islamic jurist) in response to a question posed by a private individual, judge or government.

You became ignorant of the street of my residence, ignorant of my home within you.

You were killing all the times of your longing for me by looking at the pages of large books with deep sciences.

You were shortening the time between you and me in your own laboratory, to come with a new invention, a new theory for the powerful sciences of the age, and to be outside the circle of feelings once again.

To be outside the circle of my aching heart in your absence, to be outside the semi-circle of the rainbow of my soul, to be far from the ever-shining sparkle of my eyes.

You decided to stay in your glass laboratory to astonish the world again, to fight the light of your heart spread within you, to kill the flash of lightning in it, to declare to it that I have no love revolutions within me, so that your usual youth may die in you.

How cruel it is to be silent and always wear a veil of invisibility! To be preoccupied with the concerns of the world and to forget the concerns of your soul, which is tormented by the pains of time within you, oppressed by the decisions of silence about you.

If you decide to be silent forever, then I have decided to rejoice for the rest of my life, to light inside me candles and sparkling pearls, to love you until this love kills and ends me after you. Then my longings vanish, and my heartbeats stop.

I decided to always rejoice, to draw smiles on the faces of the miserable children of the world, to plant the palms of feelings among all people who do not know whether they love or are ashamed of love.

They have not learned how to deal with true feelings.

I decided to always smile, to wear joys in winter and summer, to pour from the sun of life bright rays on the face of my sad heart, and to wash away sorrows with the water of the vast oceans, to soak my body in the autumn rains, to wash the wounds of time in it, to return to it its usual splendor.

I will leave behind a long history , mixed with tender feelings, translated into alphabetical letters.

You will sleep like the mummy of the Pharaoh in the bosom of every mind that it passed through and deposited in it.

You will enjoy it and make another human being out of it.

16

Your love shakes me like a violent earthquake

Sir.. How many wedding homelands will you free for me?

How many floating islands of pleasure will you build for me on the shores of your eagerness?

How many tokens of happiness will you give me?

What will you do with me in the future?

Will your love keep flowing?

Will you always miss me?

Will you still love me violently and adore me madly and endlessly?

Will you house me in your crystal palaces and bring me cups of tea?

Will you offer me breakfast in the French way?

By God, Reassure me that your love will never run out, tell me that I sit on the throne of your heart, that I am the only one residing it, and that I am your anticipated bride.

What will you dress me in all my moments of weakness with you?

What will you gift me in all your long nights with me?

My lord,

Your love shakes me like a violent earthquake that hits a distant city where the place is just solid rocks.

I find all my depths cracked by the powerful blows of your love. I gather everything that is in my heart to leave at the borders of your eyes.

I dwell in your terrible eyelashes, so that I can be your favorite newspaper that you bring every morning and accompany you every day and evening.

You solve the crossword table.

I wanted to live with you the autumn which makes me feel human weakness, and moves all my senses.

I feel a wild desire for everything.

I find myself in need of everything.

I find myself melting like ghee that is exposed to the heat of the summer sun.

I find myself a female to the manner born , who loves you with great passion, and panting groans because her desire for you have exceeded all limits.

How beautiful autumn is when you are with me!

How much I wished that my love story would begin in it.

I would be a woman whom you had never known before.

You would not find the like of me as long as you live.

I walk with you down the roads and streets of the city, under its tall trees that greet us with their colorful leaves in various colors.

I like to wear jeans and let the locks of my hair move with the autumn breeze.

I hold your hand and we run together raising our faces to the sky and shouting loudly, confessing our love, our longing, our eagerness.

Then I turn around in circles.

How beautiful is autumn!

This season, which puts an end to every miserable thing, renews me.

It strongly pushes me to you after it purifies me from all the filth of the world.

It washes me from the sediment of sorrows that may still cling to me.

He says to me: "This is your lover who has come to you from the farthest part in the world. He has come to you in order to open new love conquests within you."

He came to you to establish new homelands within you, in which you would make festivals of unbridled desire, which penetrated your depths months ago.

I will dress up in all the bright colors, and dance for you all the folkloric and all Arab dances.

I will move my graceful body for you like a mermaid so that I will tempt you more, so that we may complete the rituals of our feverish festival of desire.

My eyes will kill you and my graceful body will guide you to the rivers of pleasure flowing from among the rocks of severe ecstasy.

The pleasure that has no end or a separating line will remain continuous in you and devour me part by part.

It will be like an artist who enjoys coloring and coating his painting or canvas.

Thus, whenever you move the arrow of your lips, they sink into another part.

With me, you will taste sugar with all its types, you'll get drunk until you become dizzy.

You will cancel all your dates and schedule.

You will get drunk to the point of intoxication that you will be unaware of nothing but me.

You will pour on my body the wine of your heart that has intoxicated me for a long time.

Being drunk I have been searching for its components.

My lost heart pushes me towards the deserts of your flaming longings.

All your revolutions have broken out.

All your ammunition that you collected for many years have ignited.

The fuse of endless desire has exploded in you.

It has killed all misery, all silence, and all sadness within you.

You returned pure, happy and smiling like a martyr of the homeland.

You came back alive in the mood of drunkards.

You came back powerful enough to stagger over my body that was craving you.

You made me your new homes to practice your masculine dictatorship, to dive into the depth of my feminine thirst, to kill what remains of my strength.

You will creep secretly in my hungry realms at dark nights, to sow an endless night with its prestigious stars, to severe the strings connected to my heart that bind me with sorrows, fear and hesitation, to complete the journey started by our thirsty hearts.

You will occupy all the lands of my depths, without being resisted by my blood and veins.

All my cities, which I spent a long-life building, will yield to your conquering fleet.

You will be a victorious sultan in the lands of my depths.

You will plant me pomegranates, green olives, vineyards and figs.

You will construct for me gardens with flowing rivers and lakes. In my homelands, you will build your palaces and draw distinctive paintings with your lips every day.

You will color my entire body with your vivid colors.

Every day my soul will attract you to embrace and dance with it to the tunes of very quiet and romantic classical music.

You will try to live a new life in the gardens of my depths every day.

You will put an end to the routine of the diligent researcher.

You will change the course of your inflexible mind and its exhausting thinking.

By that lake and on the golden seat, you will sit looking at the distant horizon contemplating and telling our beautiful love story, playing the strings of the oud4.

You have found out the solfège on the pages of my sad heart.

It will turn me into dancing soft melodies. So, butterflies, birds, flowers, trees, wind, sea and sand will dance with me.

The clusters of your love, hanging at the top of your heart, will dance with them.

How long has love not quenched your thirst?

How long ago did the storm of love not shake you?

How long ago did your boat stop sailing?

How long ago did your heart stop beating?

How long have you been lost in a life of books, computers, tricky equations, and theories?

How long have you been away from my musical tunes?

From my letter dances?

How long have you been ignorant of my city and my rebellious style of love?

How long have I been lost in the desert of life in another woman's coat?

How long have its storms blowing at you to uproot you from your place?

____

4 The oud is a musical instrument with 10 or 13 strings , very similar to a lute.

To take you far away and strip her from her old coat?

How long have you been held hostage by a woman who, menacingly or by installments, made you love her?

How long have you been sitting in a corner of the house waiting for happiness and contentment to reach your depths?   Happiness, my beloved, is like the sun when it rises. It covers all parts of the earth.

It is not a corner of our house.

We wait for its faded rays to glow our faces.

When you are happy, you can give constant love.

You can love your kids without fearing for them.

You can give them many times what you provide for them now. When you are happy, sorrows will no longer dwell in their beautiful eyeballs or yours, either.

Also, storms of loss will never blow on their pure souls, because they are the only stars of your life, and they are the only flowers of your heart.

So, be in love and bliss!

And how beautiful it is to let your shining stars with unceasing lights embrace them tightly, play and run with them in all places.

Your flying spirit will transmit love to their spirits.

How beautiful it is to be in love, and to give love for free!

To give abundantly without stopping.

And to take the flowers of your heart and dance with them all to the dancing tunes of my love.

So, we all fly joyfully.

I love them as constantly as the succession of seasons and days, because they came from you, and carry a gene of your pure soul.

Such pure soul you came to share with me.

You came to build me a home, love, and adoration there.

They are from you, and you have brought your heart as a gift to me at the end of the year.

They are the light of your heart that illuminated the whole world.

I lightened every corner within you.

I lightened life itself for you.

How long have I been lost from my homelands and away from my planet?

How much love can make up for your deprivation?

How much love can cover your wounds or keep sorrows away from you?

How much love do you need to be free from the slavery within you?

To be free from the defeat of time within you?

To be free from the shackles of several decades that have chained you?

How much love do you need to be like a bird soaring with the eagles, conceited with the peacocks, and going wild with the lions?

How much love do you need to make us all fly to an exoplanet, so that we can all be happy?

17

The climax of longing

I always loved things that reach their climax, because I have been missing you all my life.

However, I did not know that the climax of longing is another pain and of a different kind.

Therein melodies, which I had not heard or realized before, would dance with me.

I did not know that in the solitude of my longing I would cry out my heart like a child.

I did not know that I would be stripped of the shield of joys that always protected me from the stabs of torment.

I thought that I was, by your immune love, just like a tender ballerina, flying between the earth and the sky and able to make all movements and jump freely and smoothly.

Then I would rejoice at all the times of my dancing, I would rejoice before and after my dancing .

But dancing with my heart with its warm music would ignite constant desire within you.

It would ignite fire without ashes inside you.

You would not be able to resist and endure, even in the height of the days of frost and coldness, or the snow that covers nature.

I went to search around you for my home, for my lost hugging with you.

I used to wear the light of your coming as I wear my transparent nightgowns.

So, I may seduce you and bring you to me

Then you may desire to rest your head and sleep on my breasts which were like cushions for you.

So, I may be able to contain you.

Then you might take me to a place I never knew.

Nonetheless time always steals you from me, and the place keeps fighting my coming.

The longing kept attacking me like a wild beast that never knew when to rebel?

It never knew when it would turn towards you in order to take you as prey and victim together?

I wanted to endure and wait tirelessly, to change my views, to fly through all my books, to repeat all my exams, to distract myself from passion, and from inevitable death.

Nevertheless, I would continuously collapse in a fit that would envelop my heart with your bright light.

I would collapse with every gentle touch that I needed but it didn't happen to my body.

Every night I would collapse when my bed would pull me towards it and I would find myself alone.

After that I didn't know which bed would contain you and which warmth would flirt with your depths and wrap you.

I would collapse at every kiss that had to be imprinted on my lips.

I feel that it would be given to others.

I would collapse at every letter joining me with you in writing.

As I would find it just like a mere signature to prove your presence at work in your office.

I will stop here.

I will not add a single letter because I love such messages and writings.

•••••